MW00941651

If She Can Beat Me Rockin', She Can Have My Chair!

Lessons About Life, Love, and Taking Care of Business for Young Women Today

By
Carla Ladd

An IIMS, LLC. Publication

ISBN: 9781453652404

Lessons About Life, Love, and
Taking Care of Business for Young Women Today

DEDICATION

This book is dedicated to the women who have been the most influential in my life – my mother Linda (my biggest cheerleader), my "aunt" Daisy, my paternal grandmother Minnie Sain, my dear friend Georgia Favors, my sister Casey (we wish you were still with us), and most of all my Granny – Goldie Imogene Treadwell.

Granny, you are sorely missed, but your words of wisdom live on to inspire and instruct me; to make me laugh and to make me cry. I love you and I praise God for our time together.

To all the Grandmothers, Big Mammas, Nannys, Grannys, GiGis, Mimis, MaDeas and Nannas of the world. Thank you for standing in the gap.

This book was written for all my nieces, great nieces, little cousins, and other young women who are searching to find who YOU are in an ever-changing and confusing world. You may feel like you're the only one who has ever felt the way you feel or that you're the only one going through what you're going through, but many others have trekked the same path with the same obstacles. You are not alone.

You may also think that things are so different now that old mother-wit doesn't apply today. Indeed, the world is different. However, we've all tackled the same issues, just at different times. Technology, for example, has slightly changed the way the game is played, but the game itself has not changed at all. Remember, "There's nothing new under the sun."

You are special and set apart for a divine purpose. Live up to your greatness!

My prayer for you,
First, I pray that you develop a personal relationship with our Lord and Savior, Jesus Christ. I pray that He protect and keep you always. I pray that He prospers the work of your hands. I pray that He gives you His peace in times of trouble, that you find comfort in Him in times of sorrow, and that you give Him praise for all things good.

"[You] can do all things through Christ who strengthens [you]."
~ Philippians 4:13

If She Can Beat Me Rockin', She Can Have My Chair!

FOREWORD

Ego Tripping (there may be a reason why) by Nikki Giovanni

I was born in the congo
I walked to the fertile crescent and built
    the sphinx
I designed a pyramid so tough that a star
    that only glows every one hundred years falls
    into the center giving divine perfect light
I am bad
I sat on the throne
    drinking nectar with allah
I got hot and sent an ice age to europe
    to cool my thirst
My oldest daughter is nefertiti
    the tears from my birth pains
    created the nile
I am a beautiful woman
I gazed on the forest and burned
    out the sahara desert
    with a packet of goat's meat
    and a change of clothes
I crossed it in two hours
I am a gazelle so swift
    so swift you can't catch me
    For a birthday present when he was three
I gave my son hannibal an elephant

If She Can Beat Me Rockin', She Can Have My Chair!

He gave me rome for mother's day
My strength flows ever on
My son noah built new/ark and
I stood proudly at the helm
  as we sailed on a soft summer day
I turned myself into myself and was
  Jesus
  men intone my loving name
  All praises All praises
I am the one who would save
I sowed diamonds in my back yard
My bowels deliver uranium
  the filings from my fingernails are
  semi-precious jewels
  On a trip north
I caught a cold and blew
My nose giving oil to the arab world
I am so hip even my errors are correct
I sailed west to reach east and had to round off
  the earth as I went
  The hair from my head thinned and gold was laid
  across three continents
I am so perfect so divine so ethereal so surreal
I cannot be comprehended except by my permission
I mean...I...can fly
  like a bird in the sky...

CONTENTS

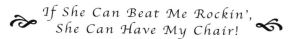

INTRODUCTION

I started thinking about this project after my dear grandmother, Goldie Imogene Treadwell, passed away in November 2001. My original intent for writing this little book was simply to document some of the wisdom and humor she imparted to me as I grew up, so that it could be shared with my nieces and the other young women in our family for generations to come. As I began to reflect on the things she taught me, I realized that not only will the young women in our family benefit from this, but other young women can also learn from these teachings and apply them to their everyday lives.

I realize that many of you more "mature" women have heard these same sayings from your mothers and grandmothers, and that much, if not all, of what Granny shared with me was handed down from generations of grandmothers before her. She probably didn't originate any of these sayings, but she certainly had a unique delivery that enabled me to recall them as I stumbled along my path. Hopefully this will bring back memories of your own mother, grandmother or special elder who guided you on your journey.

I believe that because we are conforming to more of the modern world's standards, some of this sage advice is getting lost, and our younger women are not receiving the advantage of some good old fashioned 'mother wit'.

My purpose in writing this is not to preach to, condemn or ridicule our younger women. Neither is this an all-inclusive, comprehensive guide to life or survival guide. It's simply food for thought. I'm just sharing some things that have stayed with me as I've sojourned through this life. My hope is that other young women will be edified, as I have been, by my grandmother's words of wisdom.

I intentionally left room at the back of this book for a personal note with your advice or encouragement to the young lady to whom you may later give this book.

Sharing Granny

Lessons About Life, Love, and
Taking Care of Business for Young Women Today

Before I get into some of Granny's teachings, I think it is appropriate to share a little of her story and a little of what it was like to grow up with my Granny. Born September 7, 1921 in Marion, Indiana, Goldie Imogene was the fifth of nine children born to the union of Stanley and Goldie Piatt. Her siblings were Magdelena (Maggie), Ilene, Elizabeth (Lish), Marrietta (Teddy), Stanley, Jr., Betty Louise, Phyllis and Joann.

Granny's Parents

Because of the mixed heritage of both her parents, Goldie Imogene was olive-skinned with thick, wavy black hair. Some would call this "good hair" (I hate that term). She was never a petite person. She was a sturdy 5'9" or 5'10" as an adult. She was strong-willed. She was as tough as she was pretty. She never backed down from a good fight be it with girl or boy, woman or man (when she became an adult, of course). Keep in mind that she didn't necessarily start fights, but as she would say, she was quick to end one. Everyone growing up knew that Goldie Imogene was not to be messed with.

Granny wasn't one of those super frilly, extremely feminine women (I must get that from her). She was a bit of a tomboy all her life. She wasn't afraid to get her hands dirty. She wasn't afraid of rodents or bugs (I did NOT get that from her). She wasn't always very lady-like, but she was all WOMAN.

My grandmother's education went only as far as the eleventh grade, but she was one of the wisest women I've ever known. She was a voracious reader; she read the Bible, a variety of novels, and she read the newspaper every morning. She wrote eloquent letters to her family and friends. She was good with numbers or "figures" as she called them. She had Common Sense or "Mother Wit" as some would call it, and she was a good "reader" of people. She was generous and compassionate. Granny generally loved people.

I was never told how they met, but I remember her telling me that a tall, quiet, dark-skinned man from Alabama named Grover Cleveland Alexander Treadwell "courted" her for a short while in Indiana and they married in 1940. She told me that her husband (my grandfather) said that one of the reasons  he married her was because she wouldn't "burn up his money in a beauty shop" (because of the grade of her hair). They moved to Dayton, Ohio shortly after they married.

Together, Grover and Goldie had three children: two boys, Grover, Jr. and Eugene (Monty), and a girl, Linda Sue (named after Shirley Temple's daughter) – my mother. Goldie had one son, Rodney, before she met her husband.

Grover worked as a janitor for the city courthouse and Goldie was a stay-at-home mom. Needless to say, they didn't have a lot of money. The first place of residence that Granny told me about was a three-bedroom apartment in Desoto Bass, a housing project in the West side of Dayton. Eventually, they were able to scrimp and save enough to mortgage a house in Dayton View on St. Agnes Avenue in 1965 when three of their children were still teenagers.

There is an old wives tale regarding dreaming about fish. It says that when you dream about fish, someone close to you is pregnant. Granny must've dreamt about fish just before I came into the world.

She told me that one day her daughter and a young man who was "courting" her were getting ready to go out on a date. My grandmother glared at the young man and said, "You bring Sue back here the same way she's leaving here." Although no one had said a word and she wasn't showing yet, Granny knew that her seventeen-year-old daughter was pregnant. I don't know if the young couple was contemplating aborting that child or not, but they dared not now knowing that Granny knew about the baby.

I joined the Treadwell clan in 1966 to two eighteen-year-old kids, Linda Sue Treadwell and Prince Albert Sain, Jr.

Two years later in September of 1968, my grandfather died of tuberculosis, or TB as it was more commonly called back then. After almost twenty-eight years of marriage and at the age of 47, Goldie Imogene was a widow. Granny never remarried, but she did have a boyfriend (the only one I knew of anyway). His name was Arthur. Granny always carefully watched him and other men around us kids, especially the girls. I never saw them show any affection toward one another, and he never spent the night (again, that I'm aware of). He was pretty old anyway. At least he seemed old to us kids. He was probably no older than 55-60 at the time (very young to me now).

Granny was *old school*. She didn't own a pair of pants until the mid-70s and she didn't learn to drive until well after her husband passed away. Once she started driving though, she was always on the road, and most times with us kids in tow. Boy, did she like to drive fast! Her license plate read *TREADY*, but it should've been *SPEEDY*.

Granny was never sick. Even the occasional cold didn't stick with her long. I think it was due to some of the "home" remedies she used like Castor Oil (for almost any sickness), bacon fat to draw out a splinter, gargling with Listerine (the nasty, gold colored kind) to ward off a cold, warm castor oil in the ear for earaches and many others I can't recall.

She had one remedy for baby's teething. She used to write the baby's name all over a raw egg so the baby wouldn't have trouble with teething. I have no idea where she hid the egg, but we never saw it again.

Tough as nails

I remember when I was getting ready to leave to California for college. Most of my immediate family came to the airport to see me off, including my Granny. This was before the infamous 9-11 Terrorist Attack's effect on airports, so folks were allowed to go all the way to the gate with the passengers. You simply had to pass through a metal detector. Granny let everyone else go ahead of her leaving the two of us to pass through the metal detector. Well, Granny stops me short of going through and tells me that she won't be going all the way to the gate. I ask her why not. My initial thought was that it would be too hard for her to say goodbye to her first grandchild and that she didn't want to start crying as I left her care. Not so. She told me that she couldn't go through the metal detector because of the brass knuckles in her purse. Now that was typical Granny!

Mom told me of a time when she and Granny stopped by Mom's house after being out most of the day. Granny was in her sixties at the time. Once inside, Mom noticed that the basement door was ajar. They always kept that door locked, so she knew that someone had burglarized the house. She turns to Granny and says, "I think someone's broken into the house and they may still be in here. We better get out of here." Instead of heading outside like Mom urged her to, Granny walks into the kitchen, grabs a butcher knife and heads toward the basement door. Mom grabs Granny by the arm and leads her out of the house before she could get her hands on that burglar.

A Pact with God

Granny, like many African American women, developed diabetes and hypertension (high blood pressure). By the time she was in her sixties, she was taking insulin injections and had been taking blood pressure medication for years. She had been a smoker since the age of 14, but she never had any respiratory issues besides a "smoker's cough". Granny quit smoking "cold turkey" at the age of 70. She only quit then as a bargain with the Lord. She was going to have a benign volley ball-sized tumor in her uterus removed and she called on God. She told me that she told the Lord that if He would allow her to come through the surgery and spare her a lot of pain afterward, she would give up cigarettes. God did His part and she held up her end of the bargain. She never smoked another cigarette from that day forward.

Getting her license back

When Granny was 68 or so, she had a mini-stroke that required her to spend some time in a rehabilitation center. After a few weeks in rehab, she was sent home. However, she was required to re-take the driving test to reinstate her license, yet no one would take her to practice driving.

My husband, Marion, was in town on business (without me), and he volunteered to take her driving. He calls to tell her he'll be on his way to pick her up. Granny took that to mean he was on his way RIGHT THEN. She didn't know that my husband's timing is not like her timing or mine either for that matter. After he showered and "farted around" for about thirty minutes, he heads to Granny's house. When he gets there, Granny's is sitting in the driver's seat with the passenger door open and she is steaming mad. She gets even madder when Marion tells her that she can't drive to the stadium. With a few choice words, she moves to the passenger side. After she drives around the stadium a bit, Marion feels comfortable enough to let

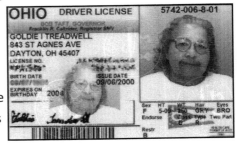

her drive back home. God bless that boy who was standing on the corner as she whipped by him on two wheels! ☺

She later got her license back and continued to drive until she was about 78, but when her hand-eye coordination started to fail, she had to stop driving. She felt as though she had lost her independence. I believe that she started to physically deteriorate from that point.

Sunset
Granny suffered a massive stroke on a late spring day in 2001.

If She Can Beat Me Rockin',
She Can Have My Chair!

My mother called to tell me. She was really shaken up, so I knew this one had to be very serious. I asked her if she thought I needed to come home. When this happened before, she told me not to come home, but this time she said yes, so I knew it was bad. I came home several times that summer to be with my Granny. I would've stayed there continuously had my job allowed for it.

Granny was such a strong woman that I believed that she would overcome this stroke. I prayed and prayed. We all did. I think once she figured out she wasn't going home anytime soon, she gave up. Her heart was so strong that she didn't go right away. I think that was God giving me time to let her go. During my last visit before she passed, I had some one-on-one time with her. That was two months before she died. She wasn't able to speak, but she was coherent. I told her how much she meant to me and how much I appreciated all that she did for me. I told her how much I loved her. A week before she passed, while I was back in Colorado, I wept as if she had already died. God was preparing me for the inevitable. My Granny passed away on November 11, 2001 at the age of 80. Goldie Imogene was the last of her siblings to transition.

Granny On...
Family & Friends
Family should take care of one another.

Family was very important to Granny. She believed that family should care for and help one another. By 1970, she was helping my mother raise her three children. Two of her own nieces, Rhonda and Terry Jo, and Rhonda's daughter Dyann were also living with her as one big family. Granny opened her home to several relatives over the years.

Granny and her siblings were close. I remember Granny taking us on short trips to Marion to visit her sisters and brother and their families. They would also make the trip to Dayton to visit us. Aunt Ilene and Teddy were the only ones who lived outside of Marion so we didn't get to see them much. They wrote to each other and kept in touch by phone.

Granny was pretty fearless. There were very few things that she feared and flying was one of them. Granny was in her sixties when she finally got the nerve to take her first plane ride to visit her sister Ilene in California. Her second and last flight was back to California for my college graduation ceremony.

Granny's was the house that every kid on the block knew they were welcome into. In the summer when we were still too young to venture out on our own, our friends would come and stay all day long on Granny's porch or we played games in the street or the backyard. Video games were still new, but Granny believed in kids getting outside for some fresh air and exercise, so we probably wouldn't have been allowed to stay inside to play video games anyway. However, when the street lights came on, we had to come inside, and "company," as she called our friends, had to go home. There were no sleepovers at Granny's house and she never felt it necessary to explain why she didn't allow it. When asked if could a friend could "spend the night", she simply said, "They have beds at their house. You'll see them tomorrow." There are several reasons why she probably didn't want our friends to stay over, three being:

1. She wouldn't rest well with someone other than her own in the house.
2. We just played all day with them, so we didn't need to sleep with them, too.
3. She didn't want to be bothered with someone else's kids all day and all night, too.

The same was true if we wanted to sleep over at a friend's house – she wasn't having it. She would say, "It would be different if you didn't have a bed to sleep in. You sleep in your own bed and see your friend tomorrow." With all the stories about child molestation, abuse and murders, I know sleepovers would definitely be a no-go for Granny in these times.

Granny had lots of friends. She knew everyone in the neighborhood and they knew her. She could remember every neighborhood kid's name. Many people would just "visit" with Granny at her kitchen table to play cards and listen to her stories and humorous sayings, though you didn't always laugh when her comments were directed at you.

Granny was very nurturing and most times sweet, but she could be brutally honest.

One of her closest friends was a lady who lived up the street, named Mrs. Wright. Mrs. Wright was deaf and blind. Almost every day, one of Mrs. Wright's children would walk her down the street to Granny's house, and the two of them would sit for hours at Granny's kitchen table 'talking'. Mrs. Wright did most of the talking, but when Granny wanted to say something to her, she would take Mrs. Wright's finger and spell out the words. It's amazing to me how long they would "talk" like that.

Just because Mrs. Wright was deaf and blind didn't mean we were excused from speaking to her when we walked into the kitchen. We were made to take Mrs. Wright by the hand and 'speak' to her. Granny didn't allow us to disrespect adults in any way.

Granny even considered it impolite for a child to call an adult by their first name. She called it, "being too familiar." We had to include "Mr. or Ms." or "Uncle or Aunt" in front of adults' names and we had to answer our elders with, "yes, Sir" or "no, Ma'am." Even as an adult, I'm not comfortable calling an elder by their first name and I still answer them using "yes, Sir" or "no, Ma'am."

Granny On...
How to Behave
(How to Act)

Granny expected us to always act like we have had "home training" whether she was around or not. She always preached that having some basic manners will take you a long way in life.

Don't be afraid to speak to people

Granny spoke to any and everybody in her path whether she knew them or not. She was known for her "Howdy do?" or "Good morning, how are you today?" She didn't care if they spoke back to her or not; she had done her part.

I am saddened by the lack of people extending this pleasantry now. It's such a simple courtesy and it doesn't cost a thing.

When you make eye contact with a person, whether you know them or not, give them a head nod or a simple, "Hello." If they return the greeting, great. If they don't, great. You've done your part. Most of the time, people will return the greeting. Don't take it personally if they don't.

It won't hurt you to be the first one to speak.

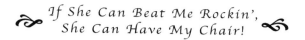

When you enter a room, give the greeting of the day.

This was one of Granny's pet peeves. She thought it was absolutely rude for a person to enter a room where other people were already gathered and not give the greeting of the day. A simple, "Hello everyone," or "Good evening everybody," is all it takes. Granny would say, "Speak behind, mouth can't," when we'd walk into a room and forgot to speak.

Speaking when you enter the room isn't "making an entrance" or "grandstanding", it's just common courtesy since you're causing the interruption to the group.

Your eyes are bigger than your belly (greedy).

When you go to someone else's house to eat, consider that other people must eat, too. Don't pile a lot of food on your plate, and then not eat it. Granny thought it insulting to waste someone else's food, especially hers. It would also be tacky to take food to-go from someone else's house (family members being the exception in most cases). Others may think it rude not to take food, but Granny thought it better to eat what you put on your plate than to take more home like you don't have food at your own house. This is especially true when it comes to more formal events like funerals and weddings.

Don't take home food from wedding receptions, funeral repasts, church picnics, etc.

Don't be so loud.

Granny couldn't stand a loud talking woman (or man for that matter). Most people have a negative reaction to the loudest person in the room. If you're not "hard of hearing," then it's unnecessary to raise your voice above everyone else's in the room. And for pity's sake, please don't yell across the room to get another person's attention. Instead, walk quickly to reach them and speak your peace.

Speak your mind, but there's a way to do it. In most cases, you don't have to yell and scream to get your point across. If someone is yelling at you, it may be best to stop talking altogether until they calm down (before things escalate).

Be confident when speaking your mind, but keep an open mind to others' opinions.

Show appreciation.

Granny would say, "The world doesn't owe you anything," so be quick to offer a word of appreciation when someone does something nice for you.   Recognize that other people don't have to be kind to you, so when they are, say "Thank You." Saying thank you won't hurt you and shows that you have some 'home training'.

A simple thank you note makes a big impression on the receiver, because a thank you note shows that you actually appreciate a person for their gift, their thoughtfulness, or their act of kindness – whatever it is. Thank you emails are okay for some situations, but on many occasions a card with a handwritten note is best. There are also occasions where a thank you gift is most appropriate.

When you receive a gift, be it for graduation, wedding, baby shower, whatever the occasion, it's appropriate and expected of you to send a thank you note. Make the mistake of neglecting to send a thank you note, and you run the risk of not getting another gift from that person.

Sometimes a thank you note isn't necessary in a casual setting like when you're invited to someone else's home for dinner. However, you should show your appreciation by bringing a dish, bottle of wine, or dessert. You can also show some appreciation for their hospitality by helping to clean up. Don't just offer to help and keep your seat when they tell you no; start clearing the dishes or putting the food away. Don't just sit back and watch the host/hostess do all the work or leave before the cleanup starts. Pitch in and help.

Follow your first mind (Trust your instincts).

Intuition is a gift we've all been given—it just needs to be developed. We develop our intuition by trusting it and acting appropriately.

Granny used to say, "Follow your first mind". She meant that our "first mind" is that initial thought that comes to mind when we're about to do something. If your mind is telling you that something just doesn't seem *right* about a person or situation, then trust your instincts and proceed with caution. Keep your eyes and ears open for warning signs. Trust the small, still voice in your head.

If your intuition or gut is telling you stop, *don't do it, danger lurks ahead*, then trust it and RUN the other way. It could save your life.

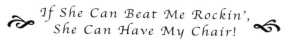

Pretty is as pretty does.

Granny used to say, "Pretty is as pretty does," whenever someone called one of her 'girls' pretty. This was to remind us that it is much more important to be pretty on the inside than on the outside.

"Pretty" is a matter of the heart. Someone attractive on the outside yet "ugly" on the inside or acting ugly, invoked this phrase from her. *Pretty is as pretty does*.

Granny didn't place much importance on outward beauty at all. To her, it was much more important to be a good person and be good to other people than to worry so much about outward appearances. Our service to others is what endears us to them, not how we look.

Selfishness is not pretty. Despite the world's philosophy of it's all about me, Granny would say, "The world doesn't revolve around you."

Don't misunderstand; I'm not saying to not look your best or to not make the most of what you're working with. There's also nothing wrong with having confidence just so long as it doesn't turn into conceit. There's nothing wrong with being known as "pretty" on the outside, so long as that is not the only thing you strive to be known for.

Granny taught me to be known as the smart, pretty girl or the girl who doesn't realize just how pretty she really is; not the girl who is always talking about how pretty her hair is, or how pretty others say her smile is, or how all the boys think she's so pretty... which leads me to another one of Granny's sayings –

Self-praise is half scandal.

Humility went a long way with Granny.

Granny thought it very rude to boast or brag on oneself. Again, there's nothing wrong with self-confidence, but when it crosses the line to arrogance or conceit, or when you begin to believe your own hype, it becomes very unattractive and downright scandalous.

Try to let your work and your looks speak for themselves. If something is notably good or if you're truly "pretty" (inside-out), others will say so. You won't have to.

God don't like ugly... and he ain't too fond of pretty either.

God doesn't like it when we act "ugly" – sin, do wrong, treat people poorly, or do anything unbecoming to Him or His glory. He certainly loves the beauty He's created in each of us, but a person's heart is what matters most to Him.

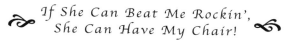

Leave something to the imagination.

Besides all the other things I mention in this book, I believe
that if Granny could offer her most important bit of advice to
young women today, she would stress that women should *leave
something to the imagination.* With the plunging necklines,
"booty" shorts, low-rise waists, midriffs and mini-skirts being
worn by young women and "not so young" women today, all her
"business" is out there for the world to see. Not too long ago,
this attire was reserved for strippers and street walkers. Now
it's hard to distinguish the "girl next door" from the prostitute on
the corner.

Is there any wonder why men have so little respect for women
when some of us have so little respect for ourselves? No decent
man wants a woman who looks like she's been "around the
block" a few times. They may want to use her sexually, but she
isn't the one *they'll take home to Momma.*

There's nothing wrong with a healthy body image, but be
careful what you're "advertising" to others. If it is not your
intent to present yourself as being easy to "get with", then dress
accordingly. It's confusing to others when you want them to
listen to your opinions and take you seriously, yet you're dressed
to bring attention to your body and not your words.

*It's hard for others to take you seriously or focus on anything
other than your body parts when you're exposing your "ASSets"*

What's done in the dark will come to the light.

Granny used to say this to us when we thought we were being slick and sneaky. She didn't always know what we kids were up to, but she was confident that if it was bad, it would come to the light eventually. I've found this to be especially true as I'm sure many of you have, too.

Here's an example. You're sneaking out of the house late at night when everyone is asleep to hang out with your friend. It's past your curfew, and your mother has told you she doesn't want you hanging out with this particular friend. After doing this several times, you think you've gotten away with it. One night, one of Momma's friends is coming in from working the night shift and sees you 'hanging out'. She calls your mother, and guess who is waiting up for you when you try to creep back into the house?

Another example. You claim to be a good church-going young woman, yet you're sneaking around having sex. After some time, you start to get sick to your stomach every day; you just don't feel right. Your worst fears are realized – you're pregnant. That fact won't stay in the dark for long.

Don't do anything that you would be ashamed of if it were broadcasted to the world.

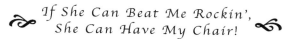

Stay out of grown folks business.

This saying has a different meaning for me now than it did when I was a child. When I was a child, Granny would tell us to leave the room when adults were talking. Sometimes I would sit around them quietly acting like I wasn't paying them any attention. When the conversation 'got good' or she noticed me 'paying attention,' she would make me leave the room.

Many parents don't do this today—they don't prohibit their children from staying in a room during adult conversations. I've witnessed people not only allowing their children to stay in the room during an adult conversation, but also allowing them to interject their comments into the conversation.

When I became an adult, this saying took on a different meaning for me. Sometimes we want to get involved when we see that our loved ones and friends are making poor choices and are heading down the wrong path. Sometimes when we offer our advice, they just don't want to hear it, and they have no problem saying just that. If and when that's the case, it's best to keep your peace and "stay out of grown folks business."

A friend of mine made a believer out of me. I practically begged her to leave a particular guy alone. Every time he would do something wrong, I would plead with her not to put up with him. Finally, I told her that I'm going to "stay out of grown folks business," and I asked her to not speak to me about him anymore. I did not want to continue wasting my time, because she was determined to be with him no matter what. I was trying to convince a fool...

I've learned to speak my peace about something important to me, and then move on if the other person isn't ready to listen. Sometimes people just need a sounding board. It's hard to just shut up and listen, but in cases like this, it's best to be still and be there for them when they finally 'get it'.

Convince a fool against his will, he's still a fool.

Don't start something you can't finish.

Granny gave me this advice when I got married; a piece of advice just for the married woman. She said, "The way you start is the way you're going to have to finish." Sometimes we women start out being and doing everything— a regular Wonder Woman. Cooking, cleaning, working 9-5, 'keeping ourselves up', you know the rest... Then as soon as we get our mate used to it and we get tired of being Wonder Woman, we try to stop. That's not fair to him. If you don't intend to continue a behavior or treatment of a person for the duration, then don't start it in the first place.

Set mutual, respectful and realistic expectations for each other in the beginning.

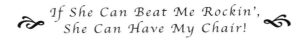

A hard head makes a soft behind.

Granny used to say this when we wouldn't heed sound advice or when we would do something in spite of her admonition not to. She said we were being hard-headed and that it would cause us pain in the long run (soft behind).

Listen and heed sound advice, especially advice from people who know and love you.

Don't let your mouth write a check your behind can't cash.

Some of us are known for being "mouthy" as Granny would call it. When we get to be about twelve or thirteen-years-old, we start "smelling ourselves" and feel we can say or do whatever we want to. We need to be reminded who is in control. Granny was quick to say, "Don't let your mouth get your butt whipped," when she was trying to be patient with us. Other times, she didn't give us a warning about the coming whipping.

This saying also speaks to making promises you know you can't keep. Don't promise to do something knowing you don't have the ability or the time to do it. If you promise to do something, do all you can to keep your promise.

Your word is your bond.

All that glitters ain't gold.

Every man that looks good, smells good, and 'acts' good isn't always good for you. We all want someone who is good-looking and is at least able to take care of himself. Most of us even want a man who knows something about God. I can testify to this. I thought that because a well-educated man I was dating could quote scripture, that he was a good, God-fearing man. He was anything but. He taught me that Satan knows scripture too.

This applies to what may look like a 'good deal' also. Take the time to investigate and pay attention to all the evidence before you commit.

Don't be mesmerized by the "bling".

You don't miss your water 'til the well runs dry.

This is one of my mother's favorites. Don't abuse, neglect, or take for granted your parents, your mate, your friends, or anything of importance to you. You'll miss them when they're gone.

Appreciate what you have while you have it.

Granny On... **Religion**

Although she was never a bible scholar and rarely quoted scripture, she taught us biblical principles through her many little sayings.

Granny wasn't a religious person, per se, but she did join the church and professed Christ as her Savior. She wasn't one of those people who "shouted" in church. When she would feel the Spirit or "get happy" as she called it, quiet tears of joy would stream down her face.

She wasn't one for long prayers from the pulpit. She called this, "begging Jesus." She believed that congregational prayer should be short and sweet and that long prayers should be reserved for your private prayer time.

On the Sundays that she didn't go to church, Granny would listen to the local gospel radio station and spend alone time with the Lord in the morning.

Get to know Jesus as your personal Lord and Savior. Salvation is about relationship with Him, not religion.

Granny's favorite scripture was Ecclesiastes 3:1-8. It has also become one of mine:

"For everything there is a season,
And a time for every matter under heaven:
A time to be born, and a time to die;
A time to plant, and a time to pluck up what is planted;
A time to kill, and a time to heal;
A time to break down, and a time to build up;
A time to weep, and a time to laugh;
A time to mourn, and a time to dance;

A time to throw away stones, and a time to gather stones together;
A time to embrace, And a time to refrain from embracing;
A time to seek, and a time to lose;
A time to keep, and a time to throw away;
A time to tear, and a time to sew;
A time to keep silence, and a time to speak;
A time to love, and a time to hate,
A time for war, and a time for peace."

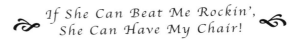

Be a good steward.

Be a good steward of everything in your possession including your time, your things, your relationships, your money and especially your body.

Time. Time is our most precious commodity, so don't waste it. Don't waste your time on idle activities that don't enrich your mind, body, soul, relationships or finances. Always keep an open mind to learning new things. Read the newspaper. Read personal development books. Read professional development books. Read biographies of people you would like to learn more about or emulate. Read the Bible. READ! READ! READ!

"An idle mind is the devil's workshop," (old English proverb). Don't waste your precious time hating on someone else with useless gossip. Don't waste your time wishing you have what someone else has (coveting). Don't waste your time on things you cannot change. Accept those things for what they are and move on to the things you can do something about. If you're jealous of your classmates good grades, then work on getting better grades for yourself. Don't spend time talking about how much you hate your job and the people you work with. Spend time preparing yourself for a better job.

"Procrastination is the thief of time." If you can knock out a task in a few minutes, what sense does it make to delay doing it? Have fun, but take care of your business first. If you need to study for a test or prepare for a presentation, then take care of that first before you go 'hang out'. You'll be able to relax and have a much better time knowing that your business has been taken care of.

Things: Take care of the things you have, but don't idolize them. Taking care of your things simply means showing appreciation for the things you already have and not stressing over the things you don't. You'll be surprised by what you gain without effort once you start appreciating what you already have and stop coveting the things you don't.

My mother always says, "Take care of your car and it will take care of you." It is essential to get the recommended oil changes, gas, and regular maintenance for your automobile. Cars can be driven well over 100,000 miles with proper maintenance.

Keep your room clean and help keep your house neat and clean, especially if you still live with your parent(s). Your parent(s) isn't the only one living there, so she/he/they shouldn't be the only one cleaning it.

Relationships: We're all very busy, but take the time to be a good steward of your relationships. Genuinely care about other people. Showing care for friends is easy. We typically call or see them often. The key thing to remember is that you have to be a good friend to have a good friend.

Nurturing familial relationships is sometimes harder. We oftentimes take for granted that our family members will be there no matter what. Call and visit your family members as often as you can if only for a few minutes, especially your elders. You can learn so much from those interchanges. Check on them. See if they need anything. Run errands for them or spend time with them. Don't do it for what you can get from them. Do it for the sake of doing it. You'll be blessed for it.

If you still have your parents, don't forget to nurture your relationship with them also. Do little things around the house without them having to ask. Do your best in all that you do to make them and yourself proud. Call when you don't need anything, and just talk. Nobody likes to hear from you only when you want or need something.

Business relationships: It's vitally important to nurture your business relationships similarly to your other relationships. Periodically send your close business associates an email just to check in. Ask about their family or inquire how business is going for them. Ask how you can support them. Always be willing to be of service to someone else. Don't just contact a business associate when you need something from them. If you contact them just because, they're more likely to return your call when you need them for something important.

Your Mind and Body: Don't cheat yourself when it comes to getting enough rest. Get your rest, but not too much rest. Six to eight hours of sleep per night is essential. Getting enough rest keeps your mind alert and your body energized. Getting too much sleep makes you lazy and sluggish.

Spend time with yourself. Spend time with God. Talk to God and LISTEN to God. To listen, you must be quiet. Quiet time in meditation is key to your mental and spiritual well-being. I spend time before I place my feet on the floor in the morning just being still. I think about the things I'm grateful for, and I thank Him for them. I ask for guidance for the day ahead and for divine protection for myself, my husband and family. In the evening, I take the time to think about the day's events and ask forgiveness for what I didn't do exactly right—for whatever I said or did that may have been hurtful. I also ask forgiveness for what I should've done, but did not do for someone else.

Take care of your body: Treat your body like the temple that it is. Don't abuse it by feeding it trash like drugs, alcohol and lots of fast food. Nourish it with good foods (fruits and vegetables) and lots of water. EXERCISE! (I fall short in the exercise department.)

Don't let anyone use your body as their sexual playground.

Don't allow anyone to physically, verbally or mentally abuse you. *Cherish yourself and others will, too.*

Granny On...
Love and Relationships

A person will only treat you the way you let them treat you.

Granny believed you have to teach a person how to treat you. She believed that if you let someone disrespect or use you, then they'll continue to do it until you stop letting them do so. You must 'nip it in the bud' right away or you're letting a negative behavior become established, and down the road, you cannot expect that person to change when you've accepted the behavior for so long.

Treat others the way you want to be treated and expect the same treatment from them.

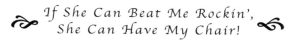

Play with trash; it'll get in your eye.

As Erykah Badu said, "Pick your friends like you pick your fruit"–
CAREFULLY. "Be careful the company you keep," Granny used to say.
At some point, your friends may be your biggest influence. Instead
of you rubbing off on them, they'll rub off on you, and bad company
corrupts.

This theme applies to all relationships. If you hang out with people
who lie, steal, fight, etc. you're bound to get in trouble just by the
association. For example, suppose you're in a store with your friend.
She decides to steal a blouse. She gets caught by security and taken
into custody. Guess what? You are taken into custody, too, just
because you are with her. The authorities don't care that you haven't
taken anything. To them, you could've been the look out. Did you do
anything wrong? Yep, you played with trash, and it got in your eye.

Here's another example. You get into a relationship with young man
you know to be a drug dealer. Yes, he has lots of money and spends
a lot on you. He takes good care of you. You want for nothing; you
think you have everything. One day, one of his rival drug dealers
decides to take out the competition, your boyfriend. You just
happen to be with him at the wrong place and the wrong time. You
both get gunned down. You're just a casualty of war. Did you do
anything wrong? Yep, you played with trash.

Hang around people who want something in life, who want to achieve something through hard work and not by taking from others.

Befriend people you can learn positive things from, who challenge you to think. A wise man once said, "Don't take advice from someone you wouldn't trade places with." Hang out with those who get better grades or who have advanced in their careers so that you can feed off their positive energy. Emulate their positive behaviors.

Don't compare yourself with your friend who "doesn't have a pot to pee in or a window to throw it out of." It's not hard to do better than her.

Birds of a feather flock together.

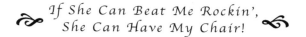
Why buy the cow when you can drink the milk for free?

Most people consider having pre-marital sex as no big deal, especially now when people are having sex without being in a committed relationship. People are also opting to live together instead of getting married. To this, Granny used to say, "Why buy the cow when you can drink the milk for free?" What is a man's motivation to marry you when he can get all the benefits of marriage without the legal commitment?

If marriage is your goal, don't offer all the benefits of marriage without the marriage license.

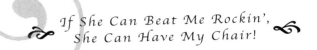
Don't chase after men.

It's no wonder younger men are so disrespectful to women. Young women can be so aggressive that they would frighten off any self-respecting man. Granny didn't believe that a woman should be an aggressor. She believed that if a man is truly interested in a woman, he'll pursue her. If he's not, he won't.

I know it's difficult to heed this advice today with the perceived 'competition' for the few available good men. Don't buy into the hype of there being a scarcity of good men. What God has for you **is for you** whether that is your mate, your job, an opportunity, or whatever. If God has pre-destined something to be yours, there's nothing anyone else can do about it, no matter how hard they may try.

What God has for you, is for you.

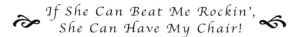
Know who wants you.

Many women, including me, have been in relationships where we wonder if our man really loves us or if he really wants to be with us. Sure, they might say they want to be with us or that they love us, but "actions speak much louder than words." What has he *shown you?* If he's not attentive to you, he disrespects you, he doesn't return your calls until he gets *good and ready,* you don't hear from him for days and then he doesn't tell you where he's been, he doesn't take you out, he doesn't take you around his friends and/or family, he breaks up with you before birthdays, Christmas or Valentine's Day, he's verbally and (God forbid) physically abusive…If he does any of these things, you don't have to guess how he feels about you – HE DOESN'T WANT YOU!

Want to know if a young man will make a good companion or boyfriend for you? Ask yourself, *is he already a good friend to me? Can I count on him to guard my secrets? Does he respect me in every way? Does he encourage me to be my best? Does he have my best interest at heart? Does he have my back? Does he like me just the way I am?*

Be friends first. If the relationship is meant to evolve into something else, it will naturally.

Before you start looking to 'fall in love', let me encourage you to fall in love with yourself first. No one is going to love you the way you deserve to be loved until you first learn to love every aspect of yourself. Learn to love your kinky hair, your big eyes, your big crooked nose, your skinny legs, and your flat butt. Work on the things you can change. If you don't like your teeth, get braces or veneers. Learn to love and embrace those things you can't change, like the big butt you inherited from your mother (thanks a lot Mom). It's all part of who God made YOU to be, but just know that He doesn't make mistakes.

The one who wants you will have your back and will treat you like the princess you are.

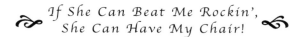

If she can beat me rockin' she can have my chair!

I'm not sure if this meant that she was confident enough in her own skills to not have to worry about her man cheating OR that she just wasn't going to waste her time worrying about whether or not he was cheating. Knowing her, I think it was the latter.

Granny didn't believe in being "jealous" of a man. She said she never worried about a man having another woman.

First of all, she believed that if a man has a "cheating heart" then he is going to do whatever he wants to do regardless of what you try to do to stop him, so why worry about it? If you know he's cheating and you're not one to share your man, then move on. If you want to stay in the relationship, that's your prerogative. But as Granny said, "He'll only treat you the way you let him treat you." Be prepared for him to continue to cheat, because by taking him back, you're saying it is okay to cheat on you.

<u>If he cheated with you, he'll probably cheat on you.</u>

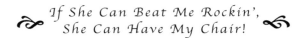

Ain't nothing like an old fool.

As we age, we should mature. We should seek wisdom. We should learn from our past mistakes and from the mistakes that others have made. Granny could excuse a young woman for being played for a fool, because young women have to learn for themselves. Unfortunately, sometimes learning to get up from a fall is part of a young woman's education in the School of Hard Knocks. An older woman should know better. "When you know better, you should do better," Granny would say. When you've seen something before, shouldn't you be able to recognize it when you see it again?

Experience is the best education.

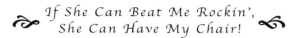

Be careful what you ask for, you just might get it.

I've heard so many young and not so young women say that they're praying for a husband. Praying for a husband is good. However, we find that many times we can't wait until God sends us one. We go searching for a husband, which is against God's rules and best intentions. His Word says, "He who finds a wife, finds a good thing and finds favor with the Lord," (Proverbs 18:22). His Word does not say, "She who finds a husband..."

Sometimes women go as far as asking God for a specific man they already have their sights set on. He may or may not be the man God has intended for you, but you've decided that he's the one for you. You beg and plead with God to help you marry that man. Ultimately, you may get the man you wanted, but without God's will and guidance in the matter, you may soon be praying for God to send him away.

Stop looking for a husband. The one God has for you will find you. Until he comes into your life, work on loving yourself.

Granny On...
Taking Care of Business

Granny was the first entrepreneur I knew personally. Besides taking care of her own grandchildren, Granny also took care of other people's kids for pay. She operated a daycare before the term daycare became popular. She just "watched" kids. People trusted Granny with their kids, even though she was a disciplinarian and didn't believe in 'sparing the rod'. Her tool of choice was the switch. For those of you who may not be familiar with this concept, a switch was a thin branch from a bush or small tree. She carried a decent sized purse, so she carried her switch with her wherever we went. Wherever you clowned, that was where you got switched. It didn't matter to her where we were – in the car, in the department store, in the grocery store. Why should she care about embarrassing you when you didn't care about embarrassing her? We couldn't call the police back then for getting a whipping. Even if we could, we would've been too afraid to do so. But, I digress...

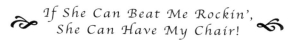

If She Can Beat Me Rockin',
She Can Have My Chair!

There's a consequence to every choice – good or bad. Choose wisely.

At some point in our lives, we must make our own choices. It is at this point that we must accept the fact that every choice we make has a consequence. Make good choices, enjoy good consequences. Make bad choices, suffer bad consequences. This applies to every aspect of your life – relationships, school, work and business. Weigh the cost of each choice you make. Think through the best case scenario and the worst case scenario. Is the best case scenario realistic? Do you want to live with the worst-case scenario? These are questions and considerations a young woman must contemplate.

It is so important to be very selective about the type of people you choose to befriend and especially the type of person you choose to have a romantic relationship with. Choose good friends, have positive influences; choose bad friends, have negative influences.

"There is no such thing as bad luck, just poor choices."
– Linda Black

Don't be that person who is always late for everything.

Granny didn't like to be late and she definitely didn't like to be kept waiting. We all know someone who is chronically late. Please don't be that person. Make your best effort to be on time for class, work, appointments and even casual meetings with family and friends. As a matter of fact, make it a habit to be a little early.

You show a lack of respect for other people's time when you can't bother to be on time. Few things bother me more than to have to wait on someone else when we have a set appointment. I feel like when someone is late, that person believes their time is more important than mine.

Granted, there are circumstances where timeliness can't be helped. But if you're going to be late, have the courtesy to call (or text), let the other person know you're running late, and give them your estimated time of arrival. Give them the option to reschedule or continue to wait.

Here are some tips I've found to be helpful for being on time for appointments:

1. When setting an appointment, always repeat the date/ time of the appointment and the location with the address.

2. Get the other person's cell phone number and give them yours just in case one of you is running late for a legitimate reason or an emergency arises and either of you need to cancel.

3. Always call the afternoon before your appointment to confirm.

You only get one chance to make a first impression. Don't let someone's first impression of you be that you are disorganized and lackadaisical about taking care of business.

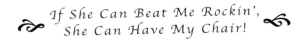
Don't cheat your time; that's lying.

Granny believed that if you'll lie, you'll steal. If you are scheduled to work eight hours, then <u>work</u> eight hours. Don't spend one hour "farting around" by talking in the break room to your home girl down the hall or talking on the phone to your friends, and count that hour toward your work time. Just because others do it doesn't mean you should do it or that you'll get away with it. Don't give the boss reason to 'trip' and potentially fire you.

Maintain good work ethic.

Granny On...
Money

I learned to live by these principles and it has saved me many headaches...

Granny never had a job outside the home, but she always had enough money to pay her bills and keep the mortgage paid. She was adamant about paying what she owed and getting paid what was owed her. **"Neither a borrower nor a lender be."** was a quote from Shakespeare's play, *Hamlet*, that Granny liked to use. If you lend it, you often won't get it back. If you borrow it, it makes you less careful in how you manage your money. Not to say that Granny never borrowed or lent money, she just didn't make a habit of doing either. She didn't give money she couldn't afford not to get back. She didn't borrow money unless she had a plan in place for paying it back. Although I had to learn this the hard way on a couple of occasions, I've learned to live by these principles and it has saved me many headaches, lost friends and lost money.

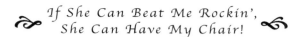

A fool and his money soon part.

One of Granny's favorite sayings was, "A fool and his money soon part." She would say this about a person who gets paid on one day, but is broke by the next, or someone who is a frivolous spender, and then has to borrow for the necessities like rent, food, gas, etc. This type of person was a fool in her eyes.

Have you ever noticed how some people always seem to have more than enough money no matter how little money they make, while others never seem to have enough no matter how *much* they make? Some people are very wise with their money. Many people are foolish with money. They spend more than they make. They borrow more than they can ever repay. They misuse credit to purchase frivolous things they want instead of waiting until they have the cash to pay for it. Most of us don't believe in delayed gratification. Hence we pull out the plastic to buy stuff we don't need. Then we "rob Peter to pay Paul" (another of Granny's regular sayings) to keep the lights on and food on the table.

Granny believed in putting away some money for a "rainy day". She had a credit card, or "charge card" as she called it, but she never kept a balance on the card and so she never paid interest. The only long-term loan she had was her mortgage. She and my mother both adamantly asserted, "Pay your bills on time!" so I would not ruin my credit.

Young ladies, please be mindful of your credit. So much depends on your credit score. A good credit score is ever so much more important now that most companies use it as a basis for employment (just like they use your criminal record). A credit score also affects eligibility for student loans.

Speaking of sensitive material for employers, in this age that we live in, be very mindful of what you post on Facebook and MySpace. Employers are using these sites as tools to investigate prospective employees.

Nobody can spend my money better than me.

Another saying of Granny's was, **"Nobody can spend my money better than me."** (Excuse the grammar). She would say this in response to women giving men their money, especially when the woman was working and the man was doing nothing to provide. Her accompanying saying was, **"I can do bad all by myself."** Granny believed that in relationships, two people should enhance one another's lives, not make them worse. She believed a man should support a woman financially. If he couldn't do that, then what good was he – just to say you have a man? For sex? Granny understood that sex ranks way up there for young women, but she just insisted that it shouldn't rank THAT high. If a man wasn't working and didn't have his own place to stay, then Granny was quick to say, "He doesn't have a pot to pee in, nor a window to throw it out of." Let someone else bear the burden of taking care of him.

Keep in mind, although Granny believed that a man should help a woman financially, she did not believe a woman should put herself in the position of being totally dependent on anyone, and this was a contemporary thought of her time. She admonished against being in a position where you need a man for your very survival. Try to be in a position where you are able to take care of yourself. That way, if your man decides to leave, you're not left "without a pot to pee in or a window to throw it out of."

Granny was speaking more from a financial perspective, but the concept applies to all aspects of life.

In all relationships, people should enhance one another's lives, not detract from them.

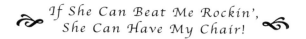
A penny saved is a penny earned.

Granny didn't know anything about investments, 401Ks, the stock
market or compounded interest (which is what *a penny saved...*
is about), but she did know how to save. More importantly, she
knew how to bargain shop, another way of saving. Granny clipped
coupons, she shopped at discount stores. There was no shame in her
game when it came to spending or saving her money.

*It's never too early or too late to start saving. Let compound
interest get to work for you ASAP.*

Pay what you owe. If you owe a debt, pay it. Integrity is an important part of character. Don't try to cheat anyone, even if a mistake on their part causes you to gain. For instance, if a cashier gives you too much change, and you know it, don't celebrate your windfall because their cash drawer is going to be short and they could get into trouble or even fired. Instead, do the honest thing and tell them of their error. Hopefully, they'll be more careful, and you'll definitely be blessed for doing the right thing. Who knows? You may be in the same position as the cashier one day. Wouldn't you want someone to show you some grace?

Be mindful, you reap what you sow.

"Waste not, want not" to me means if you don't waste or squander what you have, you won't want for anything. I said before that Granny never had a lot of money when measured by the world's standards, but she never wanted for anything. She didn't have a love of money, but she had a healthy respect for it.

Granny didn't teach us about tithing, but tithing is a very important part of stewardship. Some would argue that tithing is the most important part. I believe in tithing at least ten percent of my earnings to my church and charity. I believe in giving back a portion of what has been given to me. After all, isn't it all God's anyway?

Granny's **Humorous Side**

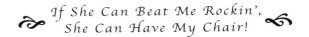

The truth is often said in jest.

Has anyone ever said something derogatory or insulting to you and then laugh it off and say, "I'm just kidding"? Well, in most cases they probably meant most of what they said. They just want to soften the blow with laughter. My mother would say, "The truth is often said in jest".

Listen for the hidden truth behind the joke.

Head looks like a chicken's butt.

One time when I was younger, Granny said this to me when I went too long without a retouch on my relaxer, and my hair started breaking off in the back. She also said it to my friends and family members when they didn't bother to comb their hair, or when they did and their hairstyle didn't meet her standards.

The fox is the finder the fart lies behind her.

Granny said this if you were the first one to notice and say something about the foul odor of freshly passed gas.

Dressed up like a Friday fart going to a Sunday meeting.

Granny used to say this when someone thought they looked good, but really didn't.

Want in one hand and pee in the other and see which one gets full faster.

You know how kids today are always wanting and begging. You hear it in the stores all the time. "Mommy I want this. Daddy, I want that." Well when we started begging, she would say, "Want in one hand and pee in the other..."

There's nothing open after 2AM but legs and 7-11.

No explanation needed. Although I've heard several variations of this saying, I'm crediting this particular one to another wise woman, Ida Gice Smith.

If you lie, you'll steal and if you steal you'll kill and if you'll kill you'll do anything. ~ Emma Gice

Granny's Famous Pumpkin Cookie Recipe

I thought this recipe was lost forever when Granny died. My mother couldn't find it until just recently, long after she stopped looking for it.

I used to beg Granny to make these cookies for me even after I grew up and moved away from home.

Pumpkin & Chocolate Chip Cookies

1 cup cooked pumpkin
1 cup Semi Sweet Chocolate Chips
1 cup sugar
1/2 cup chopped nuts
1/2 cup oil
1 tsp vanilla
1 egg
2 cups flour
1 tsp baking powder
1 tsp cinnamon
1/2 sp salt (optional)
1/2 tsp baking soda in 1 Tbl milk

Combine pumpkin, sugar, oil, egg. Stir together flour baking powder, cinnamon and salt; add to pumpkin mixture along with dissolved soda and mix well. Stir in choc chips, nuts and vanilla. Drop by spoon on lightly greased cookie sheet. Bake in pre-heated 375 degree oven 10-12 min. Makes about 5 dozen.

Wise Counsel from Other Phenomenal Women

"The way of a fool seems right to him, but a wise (wo)man listens to advice."
    ~ Proverbs 12:15

Several women of various ages and backgrounds were asked to contribute one bit of advice they would share with young women today. Here's what they have to share with you:

"Nothing is important enough to compromise your integrity." ~ Judge Glenda Hatchett – Host of Judge Hatchett Show and Best Selling Author.

"It's not always necessary for people to know what you're thinking. Sometimes, it's better to shut-up!"
~ Gloria Neal, Broadcasting Personality

"Always stay true to yourself and surround yourself with positive people." ~ Thina Johnson -President, Your Best Idea, LLC

"Listen to your inner voice, recognize your vision and let the spirit lead you to your life's purpose."
~ Charlotte Haymore – Co-founder of Travel Professionals of Color. Professional speaker, author.

"Develop an intimate relationship with God and walk in INTEGRITY daily. I always told my daughters to Listen, Think & Learn! Be lifelong learners and respect yourself." ~ Rosalyn Reese, Foto Fabulous

"Be more concerned with your character than your reputation, because your character is what you are, while your reputation is merely what others think you are." ~ Monica Campbell, Mother of two fabulous younger women.

"Get to know yourself and always love yourself. If no one else can say they love you, be able to know within you that you love you because you are somebody special."

~ Kerri Parker, Attorney

If She Can Beat Me Rockin', She Can Have My Chair!

"Always be yourself. No one can take away the beauty, gifts and talents God has blessed you with. They are yours to cherish and use to make the world a better place, whether your world is your family, your neighborhood, your city or our globe. You are special and unique. Let your light shine bright, never dimming it to make others feel better or get along with the crowd. If you are true to yourself, work hard and pray for guidance you can achieve anything you set your heart on."
~Tamara Banks-Emmy Award Winning Journalist

"Think about the most precious thing you own. Perhaps it's a piece of jewelry, maybe it's a car, maybe a pair of Nike Blazers. Whatever it is, think of how you treat that possession and magnify that treatment 100 times to determine how you should treat yourself. Then hold everyone in your life accountable for that same standard of treatment."
~ Angelle Fouther –Communications professional, Mother of two teenage daughters

"Walk on God's side, always the right decision."
~ Merriella Crowell, Entrepreneur, Marketing professional

"Like yourself and others will too..." ~ Zelda M. DeBoyes, Ph.D. - Proud Mother of two incredible women

"Best advice of all - put God first in all that you do, everything else will fall into place." ~ Elizabeth Lee

"Complete your education... it's something so valuable yet no one can ever take it away from you! " ~ Perla Gheiler, Insurance Executive

"Women are God's greatest creation. Our bodies are perfectly designed by Him as procreators of life. We bare, develop, deliver and nurture life. Therefore, we must respect and honor our bodies and make others (men) respect and honor our bodies, as well. Life does not go on without us!" ~ Paula McClain Marketing & Diversity Director, U.S. Tennis Association - Colorado District

"Have mentors. Mentors are people whose life choices you admire, be it career, style, character, etc. It is beneficial to have someone who believes in you and will hold you accountable with your choices. If there is woman whose style, attitude, career, etc. you admire, don't be afraid to talk with her to find out what she did to get that way." ~ Hanifah Chiku – Concerned Sistafriend

"The only way to realize your dreams is to wake up." ~ Joni Caldwell

"Sometimes it is hard to talk to your parents or guardian, so find an adult who you can look up to and who you trust. Ask that person if he/she will act as a mentor or sounding board for you, and if so, be honest when you talk to this person." ~ Mary Ann Townsend

"A guy who has it on the ball will only commit to a girl who has it on the ball. The converse should also be true. One who has it on the ball is maximizing her education, rocking her job, minding her money, and making healthy lifestyle choices. If he isn't doing that much for himself, leave him where you saw him. Only Jesus saves, Beloved." ~ Leanne

"Carefully select "your" goals and stay focused on the Lord." ~ Murl's Pearls of Wisdom

"Stay focused on your education and career. Don't let anyone lead you down the wrong path." ~ Margaret "Ree" Moore

If She Can Beat Me Rockin', She Can Have My Chair!

"Know your worth! Never let a man think you think more of him than he does of you." ~ Debra Jackson

"Do not be lead astray by what appears to be popular. Listen to your inner voice and make the decisions that show you know your true value and self worth. Do not let anyone else set a lesser value for you than what you deserve." – Patricia Houston, Founder and Executive Director EspeciallyMe™

"Do not let circumstances define you, you always define yourself." - Hon. Elbra Wedgeworth, Chief Government and Community Affairs Officer Denver Health

"Be a woman of your word. Once you are labeled a liar people will not trust you. Sometimes the truth hurts, but look deep inside yourself to find the tact or humor to tell someone the truth. They will forgive you for telling them the hurtful truth, but they will never forget you if you lie." ~ Lisa Young

"I try to pay attention to everything around me. There are lessons and messages from God in everything from nature to advice from a man at a bus stop to negative experiences." ~ Makisha T. Boothe, The Black Consortium

"Be strong, full of conviction and never allow your significant other to control you - no matter what. Love is wonderful but, self respect will take you even further." ~ Elizabeth (Cissy) Testerman

"Listen and promote things that will cause positive changes and have faith in God." ~ Georgia "GiGi" Favors

More to come...

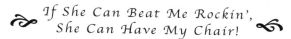
If She Can Beat Me Rockin',
She Can Have My Chair!

Recommended Reading

Below is a list of books that should be added to your personal library.

The Payton Skyy Series of books for high school girls by Stephanie Perry

7 Habits of Highly Effective Teens by Sean Covey

7 Habits of Highly Effective People by Stephen R. Covey

The Maxwell Leadership Bible

Be U: Be Honest, Be Beautiful, Be Intentional, Be Strong, Be You! by Mary Mary

Reallionaire – Nine Steps to Becoming Rich from the Inside Out by Farrah Gray

Everything has a Price – If You Have the Strength to Survive, You Have the Power to Succeed! by Veraunda I. Jackson

The Gospel of Good Success by Kirbyjon H. Caldwell

Rich Dad, Poor Dad by Robert Kiyosaki

Notes